Flies and Maggots Are Gross!

Leigh Rockwood

PowerKiDS
press

New York

Published in 2011 by The Rosen Publishing Group, Inc.
29 East 21st Street, New York, NY 10010

First Edition

Editor: Maggie Murphy
Book Design: Ashley Burrell
Photo Researcher: Jessica Gerweck

Photo Credits: Cover © www.iStockphoto.com/Frank Hatcher; pp. 4, 5, 6, 8, 9, 10, 16, 17, 18, 22 Shutterstock.com; p. 7 Dr. Richard Kessel & Dr. Gene Shih/Getty Images; p. 11 © www.iStockphoto.com/ Jaroslaw Wojcik; pp. 12, 13 (bottom left, bottom right) Frank Greenaway/Getty Images; p. 13 (top) Wikipedia Commons; pp. 14–15 © www.iStockphoto.com/Carlo Fiumana; p. 19 Photo by Scott Bauer/Courtesy of the USDA; p. 20 NHMPL/Getty Images; p. 21 Will Heap/Getty Images.

Library of Congress Cataloging-in-Publication Data

Rockwood, Leigh.
   Flies and maggots are gross! / by Leigh Rockwood. — 1st ed.
      p. cm. — (Creepy crawlies)
   Includes index.
   ISBN 978-1-4488-0703-1 (library binding) — ISBN 978-1-4488-1367-4 (pbk.) —
ISBN 978-1-4488-1368-1 (6-pack)
   1. Flies—Juvenile literature. 2. Maggots—Juvenile literature. I. Title. II. Series: Rockwood, Leigh. Creepy crawlies.
   QL533.2.R63 2011
   595.77—dc22

                                                  2010010299

Manufactured in the United States of America

CPSIA Compliance Information: Batch #WS10PK: For Further Information contact Rosen Publishing, New York, New York at 1-800-237-9932

Contents

Filthy Flies.. 4

True Flies... 6

Fly Species....................................... 8

Fly Habitats 10

Life Cycle 12

Fact Sheet: Gross!..........................14

Fly Food 16

Fruit Flies.......................................18

Black Flies 20

Shoo, Fly!.......................................22

Glossary 23

Index 24

Web Sites..24

Filthy Flies

Many people are grossed out by flies because they know that these **insects** can spread germs and dirt wherever they land. When a fly lands on your food, its feet carry matter from where it last landed. The last place that a fly landed might have been trash or even animal waste!

▼ When many people think of flies, they think of the common housefly, shown here. However, there are more than 100,000 species of flies in the world!

Maggots, shown here, look like tiny, wiggling white worms. Maggots do not have legs.

Flies do other gross things, too. When they land on food, they spit on it. Their spit then breaks down the food so they can suck it up through their mouthparts. Flies lay their eggs in trash, animal waste, or on dead animals. When the eggs hatch, wiggling **larvae**, called maggots, come out to feed. They grow into flies.

Some insects, such as dragonflies and fireflies, have the word "flies" in their names. However, some of these insects are not true flies. True flies are a group of insects that includes the mosquito, the gnat, the fruit fly, and the housefly.

Like all insects, true flies have six legs. Also like all other insects, true flies' bodies

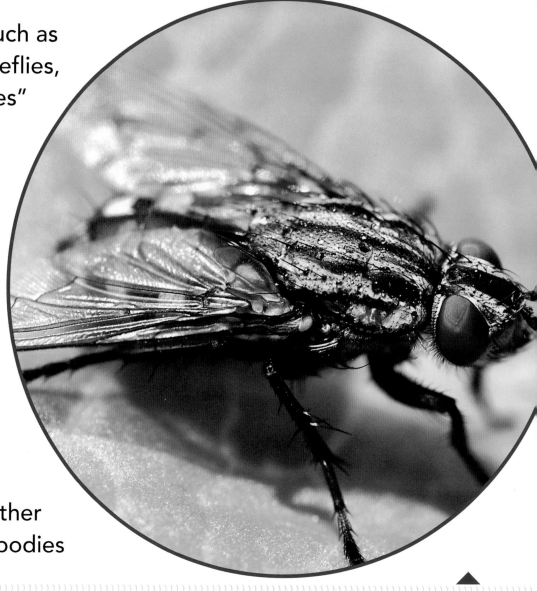

True flies make up an order, or group, of insects called Diptera, which means "two wings" in Latin.

Here, you can see a close-up picture of one of a fruit fly's compound eyes.

are divided into three parts. Flies have heads, **thoraxes**, and **abdomens**. As a group, true flies have a few things in common. They have one pair of wings. They have tubelike mouthparts that they use to suck up food. True flies also have **compound eyes**. These are large eyes made up of hundreds of tiny simple eye parts.

Fly Species

There are tens of thousands of **species** of flies. The smallest are midges, which are about .05 inch (1 mm) long. The biggest are robber flies, which are up to 3 inches (8 cm) long. Houseflies are somewhere in between, at around .3 inch (8 mm) long.

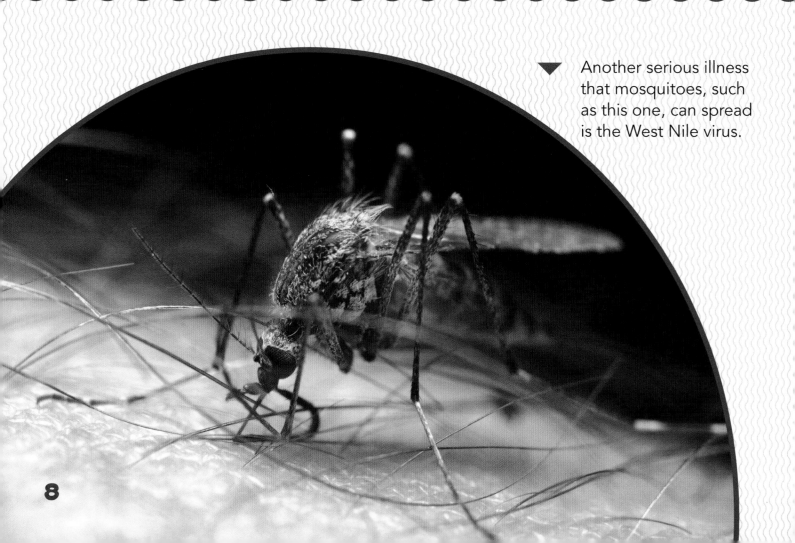

Another serious illness that mosquitoes, such as this one, can spread is the West Nile virus.

Fruit flies are a species of tiny tan and brown flies. They generally have red eyes, as this one does.

Flies spread many different illnesses. Some species, such as mosquitoes, bite people and animals. Many others species spread sickness because they bring germs from trash and animal waste wherever they land. Mosquitoes spread malaria and yellow fever. Tsetse flies spread African sleeping sickness. Even common houseflies can spread cholera and typhoid. All of these illnesses can be deadly.

Fly species are found in most parts of the world. However, fly eggs and maggots grow best in warm, wet **habitats**. This means that there are generally many flies buzzing around in the summer or in places that are warm year-round. Flies are very active during the day. At night, they rest on outdoor wires,

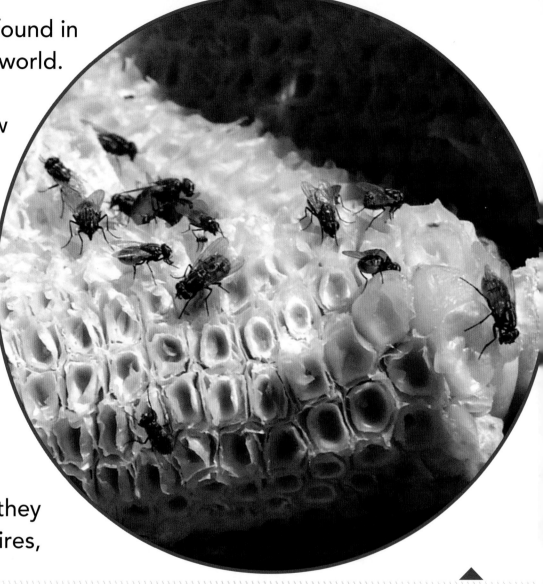

You will often see flies feeding on food and trash, such as this group of flies feeding on some corncobs.

Maggots sometimes feed on live animals, such as sheep. This can hurt the animals and even kill them.

tree branches, and on ceilings inside houses. Most flies stay within a few miles (km) of where they were born. Flies also stick close to places where they can find food, whether that food is rotting trash or food left out in the kitchen.

Life Cycle

2

The maggots then enter the **pupal** period. In this period, a hard shell forms around them while they grow into adult flies. After they have grown into adults, the flies break through the pupal shells using bumps on their heads. These bumps then disappear.

1

Houseflies hatch from eggs as white, wormlike maggots. The maggots grow quickly and **molt** three times as they grow. After the third molt, maggots dig into the matter on which they are living.

Adult houseflies can sometimes live for a few weeks or months if they are lucky enough not to get swatted or eaten by another animal. However, these flies can only live for two or three days without any food.

Houseflies spend most of their lives by themselves. They come together only to **mate**. After mating, the female fly lays eggs. She lays them on a supply of food for the maggots that hatch from the eggs. Maggots hatch from the eggs within a day.

3

1 Many species of flies live through the winter by staying in the egg or remaining in the pupal period until spring.

2 Most flies feed only during the day. However, maggots eat all day and all night.

3 Some flies have suction cups, called pulvilli, on the bottoms of their feet. These suction cups allow the flies to land anywhere, even on walls or ceilings.

4 Females of some species of flies lay their eggs inside larger insects or spiders. Once they hatch, the maggots start to feed on that insect or spider while it is still alive!

A housefly's wings move at about 200 to 300 beats per second while it is flying.

5

Many fish like to eat wiggly maggots. People who go fishing often buy maggots to use as fish bait.

6

The Venus flytrap is a plant that eats flies. When a fly lands on it, it gets stuck on the plant's sticky leaves. The leaves then close around the fly.

7

Doctors sometimes use special maggots to clean deep cuts. The maggots are used to eat dead tissue so that healthy tissue can grow.

8

Fly Food

Flies smell food around them using their **antennae**. If something smells good, they fly over to have a taste. Flies taste food using both their feet and sense organs on their heads called palps. However, flies do not have teeth, as many other animals do. Instead, they have mouthparts made

▼ Here, a robber fly sucks the insides of another insect through its mouthpart, called a proboscis.

Insects, such as flies, are often food for spiders once they have become caught in a spider's web.

up of a strawlike tube with a mouth at the end. These mouthparts make it easy for them to eat liquids. Flies eat solid food by spitting on it. This spit breaks down the food enough so that it can be sucked up.

Many animals eat flies and maggots. Birds, frogs, and other bugs are among the animals that eat flies. Spiders also eat any flies that are unlucky enough to fly into their sticky webs.

17

Have you ever reached for a piece of fruit and seen a bunch of tiny bugs flying around it? Those bugs are likely fruit flies. Adult fruit flies are about .125 inch (3 mm) long and have red eyes. Fruit flies and fruit fly maggots live on ripe fruit and vegetables as well as on trash in trash cans. Gross!

An adult female fruit fly can lay about 500 eggs at a time.

Fruit flies lay their eggs near the surface of ripe or rotting fruits and vegetables. These fruit fly maggots have hatched in a piece of fruit called a papaya.

Fruit flies grow from egg to adult in about a week, and their adult lives last only a few more days. It is easy to study fruit flies for their whole lives because they have such a short life cycle. That is why some scientists use fruit flies in their studies. Fruit flies are best known for their use in the study of **genetics**.

Black Flies

Here you can see a black fly's compound eyes and antennae.

People often see swarms, or big groups, of black flies when they are in woodsy places in the spring and summer. These black flies are small. They are only about .125 inch (3 mm) long, but the females have a nasty bite. The females bite people and animals to drink their blood. This gives them the energy they need to lay their eggs.

Male black flies feed on flower nectar, rather than on the blood of mammals, as females do.

Black fly eggs hatch in running water, such as streams. The maggots hang on to rocks and other objects in the water. A group of black fly maggots looks like wiggling moss in the water. Black flies spend the pupal period in the water, too. Adults fly away from the water to mate and feed.

In many ways, flies and maggots are annoying or dangerous pests. Flies spread germs that can make people sick or even kill them. Some species of flies give painful bites to people and animals. Maggots can ruin fruits and vegetables.

Flies and maggots are gross and can spread illnesses. However, they also play an important part in life on Earth.

Flies and maggots are also an important part of many **food chains**. Maggots and flies are food for many different animals. When maggots feed on dead animals, they are breaking down those animals' bodies. In time, this returns **nutrients** to the soil and helps plants grow.

Glossary

abdomens (AB-duh-munz) The large, back parts of insects' bodies.

antennae (an-TEH-nee) Thin, rodlike feelers on the heads of certain animals.

compound eyes (KOM-pownd EYZ) The larger eyes of bugs, which are made up of many simple eyes.

food chains (FOOD CHAYNZ) Groups of living things that are each other's food.

genetics (jih-NEH-tiks) How features are passed from parents to children.

habitats (HA-buh-tats) The kinds of land where animals or plants naturally live.

insects (IN-sekts) Small animals that often have six legs and wings.

larvae (LAHR-vee) Animals in the early period of life in which they have a wormlike form.

mate (MAYT) To come together to make babies.

molt (MOHLT) To shed an outer skin. This allows an animal to grow.

nutrients (NOO-tree-ents) Food that a living thing needs to live and grow.

pupal (PYOO-pul) Having to do with the second period of life for an insect, in which it changes from a larva to an adult.

species (SPEE-sheez) One kind of living thing. All people are one species.

thoraxes (THOR-aks-ez) The middle parts of the bodies of insects. The wings and legs come from the thorax.

Index

B
bodies, 6, 22

E
egg(s), 5, 10, 12–14,
  19–21

F
feet, 4, 14, 16
food, 4–5, 7, 11–13,
  16–17, 22
food chains, 22

G
genetics, 19
germs, 4, 9, 22
group(s), 6–7, 20–21

H
housefly, 6, 8–9,
  12–13, 15

I
insects, 4, 6, 14

L
larvae, 5

M
mosquito(es), 6, 9
mouthparts, 5, 7,
  16–17

N
names, 6

P
part(s), 7, 10, 22
people, 4, 9, 15, 20,
  22
period, 12, 14, 21

S
species, 8–10, 14,
  22
spit, 5, 17

T
thoraxes, 7
trash, 4–5, 9, 11, 18

W
waste, 4–5, 9

Web Sites

Due to the changing nature of Internet links, PowerKids Press has developed an online list of Web sites related to the subject of this book. This site is updated regularly. Please use this link to access the list:
www.powerkidslinks.com/creep/fly/